# THE SINKING HULK

n a r a y a n i

ISBN: 978-93-5980-188-9

Second edition 2023

Dedicated to

The ones who acknowledged me when no one else could and trusted me and my dreams even when I couldn't.

*Deepasha Narayan*

and

*Aashish Dangi.*

# Acknowledgments

My deep gratitude also goes to *Deepasha Narayan* for this beautiful book cover, and *Ashwin Ramesh* and *Aparna Garg* for your belief in me and my work.

A heartful thanks to *Jameela Kagzi* for beautiful illustrations, *Varun Verma* for the author's picture and every technical help, and *Cassia Hall* for editing guidance.

A special thanks to a friend and psychologist, Ms. *Kamakshi*, for her kind guidance and meaningful words for this project.

# Preface

Dear Reader,

Thank you for picking up this book. Before you start reading, I want you to take a minute to connect with the emotion in every word you will be reading in this book.

Remember when you achieved something, no matter big or small, you were acknowledged by someone. This same person was by your side when you were struggling or failing again and again before you succeeded.

Who was that person? ______

What was your relationship with that person?

______

Dedicate this reading to this person for whom your failure and achievements were this important, the person who loves you unconditionally and supports you, and whose guidance is so valuable to you.

No doubt, their success excites you too, and you smile when they are happy or achieve something.

But have you ever imagined how it feels to see that person crying or falling apart for some reason?

Have you ever felt the helplessness of seeing the strong wall supporting you slowly becoming brittle?

Share your experiences with me. I will be waiting for your response.

Also, I would love to know your experience of reading *The Sinking Hulk*.

*Narayani*
(e-mail: narayani0505@gmail.com)
(Instagram: @narayani_aura

# The Sinking Hulk

Under the blue sky,
I see you lying.
You are gazing at the clouds,
turned white after the rain's demise.

I stay quiet,
witnessing a serene state,
air is playing with your hair.
It is so beautiful to see, so fair.

## The Sinking Hulk

Surely, the fragrance of moist soil,
beneath the clear sky's expanse,
enriches your spirit and toil,
bringing relief to every pore, perchance.

Seated by the window bay,
I see you closing your eyes.
I see the purity in your innocence,
fallen on the concrete dais.

You've always been my love,
but sensing your calm like this
enhances my peace.
I rest, it's a moment to celebrate.

Yet why do your toes turn rigid?
from nowhere, this sudden change.
Your clenched fist seems frigid,
confusion in this moment strange.

# The Sinking Hulk

Surrounded by a million questions.
I rise, but my steps are falter.
Tears stream for your eyes' expressions,
Cascading down on either altar.

Your fist is struggling to rule the brain,
your teeth grind against hidden pain,
and I see you motionless and still…
as if someone has pierced my every vein.

Was that just me, wearing the glass of right?
because reality is making your eyes wet.

# The Sinking Hulk

I brawl with myself,
collect the torn pieces,
and stand up, trashing all my glasses,
to see the bitter truth, no less.

I kept an eye on your growth.
Did my barriers prove weak?
That pain easily broke through
leaving scars that we seek.

I sit next to you,
claiming you are not alone
but the wall remains visible to me,
you just smile and say, 'I know.'

You've learned to hide the pain,
while I'm feeling caged.
I want to ask, but fear to hurt,
afraid of crossing the delicate line.

I glance at the pictures, memories so clear,
from our last trip to the tranquil lake.
Shining eyes and laughter near,
I miss the days when you were not fake.

I seek every reason
for your pain and tears.
Money, exams, or peer
I go through every shoe you wear.

I speak to your friends, seeking solace,
to make me feel prepared.
I'm resolute in unravelling hidden distress,
to know the depth of fear, truth at its best.

Our words extend beyond spoken tales.
Our bond transcends months and years.
I may not believe in fate
yet destiny has chosen you, my mate.

I yearn to comprehend your every pain.
Baby, we were born to be one another's tail.

# The Sinking Hulk

I know I have to do this.
But how? I'm still unsure.
I envisioned you in eternal glee,
this situation, unforeseen and obscure.

***

Yet I recall the day vividly,
donned in a black skirt
and floaters blue,
I was desperately looking for you.

I ran to you when I saw a bundle of love
You were an infant wrapped in a towel
asleep in Father's arms.
All I could see of you were your tiny feet.

I jumped up to have a glance.
When the nurse came,
Father had to fetch some medicine near,
I got to hold you, my precious, so dear.

I remember Father said,
'Baby is so little, so delicate,
so, make sure you take care.'
I didn't think once to say,
        'Baby, I'll keep you safe always.'

You were sleeping calmly in my lap.
Your skin a plum-red, soft, and tender,
I was touching you with so much care,
like you were a petal of fragile aster.

# The Sinking Hulk

Your heart was beating so fast,
A darker tongue nestled amidst petals,
Long eyelashes adorned your peaceful rest,
I was waiting for you to wake up…
I also wanted to be seen.

I didn't know
if you were a boy or girl
but when you opened your eyes,
held my finger, you were my whole world.

***

How can I falter` at this moment anyway,
I remember what I said,
'I'll keep you safe always.'

This day has arrived again
I run towards you.
We will mend every wrong together,
Assuring you, we'll find the right way.

I knock on your door
seeking your heart's shore.
Sitting beside you, my presence assured.
I'm with you from my core.

# The Sinking Hulk

Uncertain of where to begin, how to start,
I don't know what to ask,
but when you ask my purpose
All I say is, 'How are things in your life?'

You laugh a little,
I feel so insane.
'All good, everything is smooth,
except for law and maths,' a lie, in truth.

‘If you need help,
I’ve a friend with expertise.’
Is that my best shot
to break the ice?

‘No… No need to worry,
I’ll manage somehow.’
You have grown up so fast, baby,
these words made me realize.

I gaze at you, amazed, and dazed,
your voice deepened; facial hair grazed.
Puberty's changes, not just physical in scope
I see the burden you carry, weight of hope.

Emptiness resides within your eyes,
You think you know all, yet this is the guise
Honey, it's just the beginning,
there is so much more to discover.

I am proud you are growing so well,
but you need to know, a family shares all pains.

# The Sinking Hulk

You smile
with some resistance.
Your eyes are lowered
but dude, I'm your elder sister.

'Want some noodles?' I ask in jest.
'Don't want to die,' you say with a frown.
I know my skills in the kitchen,
also, how to lighten your heavy heart.

## The Sinking Hulk

Long time after
We cook together.
Though I stand aside
still claiming, 'I cooked' as a tether.

We break down in the pan itself
before the noodles stuck, our chaos began.
So many things can never be changed,
like your burp after chopsticks are estranged.

The sky is again cloaked in dark clouds.
Staring up, while you seated on the ground.
Plafond of lighting and thunder roar,
I hope you say what's inside your core.

I rest my head on your belly,
and let the rain drench our bodies.
Celebrating the music of rain's refrain.
synching with the rhymes of air's domain.

The flow of wind rules the pattern,
but wavy water reaches satisfaction.
Feeling the pleasure of every drop
to get to the earth after a long war.

I see you closing your eyes,
no pain but just a calm smile.
Your peace remains pure as a little child.
Puberty can't take away your innocence.

I may not comprehend the struggle you face,
but 'We' are important for the soul's grace.

# The Sinking Hulk

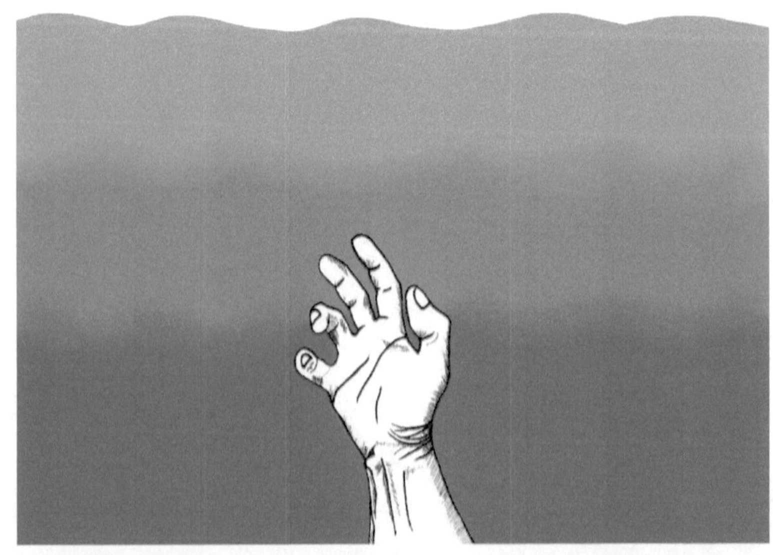

Asking you about it,
I don't know if it is right.
I just celebrate the moment,
with our cute siblings' fight.

We run together,
we shout like kids of eight or nine.
Laughter carries us to a warm hug.
It is precious to relive as a child.

# The Sinking Hulk

I hold myself back a lot,
but can't help these tears.
'Do you trust me?' I ask confronting fears,
you notice the dampness on your shoulder.

You hold me tight with both hands.
I can tell you are so worried.
'I know you are not happy… I can sense.'
You gaze at me wearing a knowing grin.

'I am now taller than you
yet, you treat me like a little child.'
I fall silent,
awaiting the truth, meek and mild.

You turn away, breaking our shared gaze.
I rest my head on your shoulder's embrace,
wrapping my arms around you,
turning you to look at me.

You hold back your tears.
I have much to say but end up with a few,
'I respect, if you need your time,
but this time, please don't lie.'

I see the trust in your gesture,
confidence emanates in your posture,
your eyes glistens again.
I hope this radiance lingers and remains.

I know something is piercing you,
but hope now you know, I'm always there.

# The Sinking Hulk

Days pass, and I witness your pain,
though you try to hide, it's in vain.
My efforts long for recognition and care.
When will you count on me and share?

But this day, as I approach your side,
I witness you hurting, losing your stride.
your head hangs low, gasping for air,
frantically scratching your dishevelled hair.

I rush to embrace you in my arms.
It is not teen stress, it's self-hatred blight.
It's like a part of you has been lost,
self-love and self-worth, now tempest-tossed.

I hold both of your hands
and feel your clenched fists.
You rest your head on my lap
while tears in your eyes persist.

'I hate myself,
I can't trust my mind.'
you curse yourself,
it stabs at my heart, unkind.

I wipe your dripping nose,
and tears from your face,
I want to understand,
And offer you solace.

I hug you tight,
my fingers caress your head.
'I can't leave you alone in this fight,
speak freely, for I see it in your eyes.'

You struggle for the breath,
and collect the shattered, to speak.
You gasp for breath till you grip my hand
but when it comes to my eyes, you can't see.

'What if you too hate me, I can't say.
Your love is precious, I can't lose it anyway.'

# The Sinking Hulk

I look around,
finding no way.
I don't know how to calm you down.
For this, I was never prepared.

I keep asking, what's the matter?
I wonder if you regret something,
I doubt if you have committed some sin,
Are you on the path of those sinners I met?

'What is the reason for such a rase?
Why can't you trust yourself?'
'Are you hurt or have you hurt someone?
Tell me baby... what have you done?'

'Nothing... I've not done anything wrong.'
I breathe a moment of calm.
'But I can sense a demon of being a man,
what if I hurt any innocent someday?'

'Demon? What are you saying?
Stop saying rubbish
and puke out what's in your mind.'
I can't get what he wants to say.

'How can you not understand?
You know man.
Man… who knows how to betray,
Man… who even made you cry.'

I freeze and you keep saying
'I can't trust manhood,
I know your fear, your pain.'
I don't know why you are saying that.

What made my incidents descry?
I don't know when you see that all.
For now, I keep hugging you,
until you sleep on my thighs.

I smiled all the time, hiding my tears,
and today, I'm the reason for your fear.

You sleep quietly,
evoking my harrowing fight.
The teen is meant to be the age of learning,
but like you, I was bearing my fears.

I never thought you knew,
I sewed my lips,
I didn't dare recall it myself,
and buried that day in my heart.

## The Sinking Hulk

It's been so many years
still, I'm caged with the same fear.
That was scary...so bad,
and you know, this is making me mad.

I've lain next to you,
and keep staring at the ceiling.
I can hear those suppressed screams,
those I hid till now in the name of healing.

I was a small girl,
of twelve or thirteen,
when that monster showed up,
and took away all my peaceful sleep.

***

I was peddling back from school,
and he followed me, maybe for so long.
He blocked my path
and asked for a way.

I pointed him to the road.
he stood adjacent to me... so close,
and then praised my long braids.
I mounted my cycle back to go home.

He lifted it up from the surface,
I fell down, my knee got grazed.
I looked at him with anger,
when he showed me his true face.

***

Those were the moments of terror,
even after twelve years, I still feel that fear.

# The Sinking Hulk

***

He bent to grab me,
I looked around and 'Help!' I shouted,
but doors remained shut,
under the May's scorching sun.

I ran to retrieve my bag,
but he broke my ride before I could pick.
That man with grey hair is on a yellow bike,
wearing his cop's uniform and shoes brown.

His smile was so vile. He gripped my neck
and pushed me against the wall.
I looked into those evil eyes,
begging to awaken his mercy side.

He forced my hand,
to touch some warm flesh down.
I tried to withdraw,
but he choked me by clutching my neck.

He spat on my palm,
I reacted with such disgust,
by kicking him on his shin.
He made it move there fast.

I struggled for every breath,
while he bent to kiss my neck.
I struggled to get rid of his touch.
I didn't know what was happening so much.

## The Sinking Hulk

He released me,
with some warm fluid
over my fingers. I tried to run,
he dragged me by scratching my hair.

He pushed me to the floor
and tried to poke that dark in my mouth.
It was huge and horrible,
It was just disgust.

'Don't,' I shout, 'My father will kill you.'
'If you tell him, he'll only blame you.'

# The Sinking Hulk

I closed my eyes,
and pushed him hard,
with the strength of all life,
to see him finally fall on the path.

I ran out of there
while he leaned against his bike.
I reached the road
and saw a crowd.

## The Sinking Hulk

I sat on the pavement against a wall
and gasped. My eyes were flowing
when a lady asked,
'Are you injured or something you want?'

I looked at my knee
while wiping my tears.
My hand was stinking
from the fluid that had appeared.

She helped me to stand.
It was the wall of *gurudwara,*
she took me in,
where I washed my fingers and knee.

She comforted me,
and gave me first aid.
I asked her to help me.
She walked along to get my bike.

# The Sinking Hulk

I reached home
with so much pain in my heart.
I had a lot to say, I wanted to cry,
but I was late, so heard my mom's shout.

She never showed her trust in me.
'She won't listen,' I thought.
I kept quiet and got scolded all time.
I slept early before my father came.

I got a number of chances, to share,
but that man's words pierced me...
after that, I was not ready to be blamed.

***

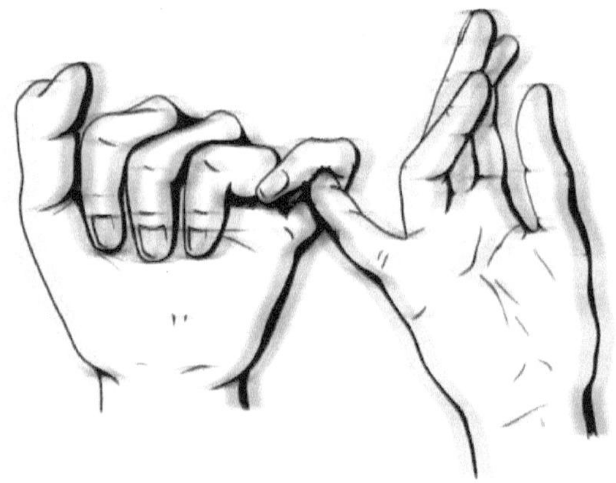

Today, you are sleeping here,
with your head on my arm.
I've left all that behind, so far.
Maybe because I was a coward.

It was difficult for me
to explain what happened.
I couldn't face my own family.
Somewhere, I was blaming myself.

# The Sinking Hulk

I didn't see trust
for myself, in eyes of my people.
I saw love and care
but failed to seek belief in me.

I never felt safe
at home, the makers have earned.
So much comfort I had,
but couldn't see the concern.

Baby, years ago... I held you
and promised to keep you safe.
I heard your fears,
I trusted your potential.

I never withheld my support,
encouraging you to dream and court,
to strive for greatness, reach the sky
and claim what's rightfully yours, oh so high.

## The Sinking Hulk

I sheltered you when storms drew near,
and let you face challenges, without fear.
My hand was always there to grasp,
to remind you that I'd never lapse.

I simply longed to witness,
that self-trust in your eyes, again.
You to realize, you have earned belief.
You to realize, you have people for life.

All I wanted you to have a home,
to feel safe but I guess, I failed.

# The Sinking Hulk

I spend time
to know more in you.
It is the terror
if one gets hurt by you.

You say I can't understand your strife.
Yet you hide, avoiding life's rife,
instead of standing tall, making amends.
It is so wrong... I know by myself.

You want to hide now,
leaving society behind
but you couldn't learn to bike,
unless you go for a ride.

I counsel you.
I use examples with care.
I appreciate the kindness,
and sensitive heart, you inherently bear.

But you are stuck at a point
'What if I do something that I should not.'
I can't know why don't you understand,
being cruel is not meant for your soul.

I was hurt by a man,
so never wanted you to hurt anyone
but I never expected
you to torture your own heart.

# The Sinking Hulk

I thought to keep you occupied.
I keep you engaged with some games,
I help you study,
and distract you with some lame.

But yes, such measures are transient,
not forever.
seeking enduring peace,
an endeavor to endeavor.

The radiance and grace that once were vivid,
Now veiled, subdued, a predicament insipid.

# The Sinking Hulk

Feeling like...I am useless here.
I want to share my fear.
Can I seek Father's invention,
to navigate this trying situation?

I believe he can handle
way better than me,
but it took a lot of you
when it came to sharing with me.

# The Sinking Hulk

I look at our parents' faces,
tired and worn,
but I know, I can't take it forever,
this is what I have to do.

I sit beside my Dad
and try to know his concern
'Is everything okay with brother?
Don't you think he is disturbed or stressed?'

His response echoes in laughter,
and says it is just a phase.
Teenage is meant for learning,
that gives us situations to face.

He has no idea what kind of situation
this age has given to a little mind.
How unguided learnings
can inflict such strife.

# The Sinking Hulk

He is not ready to explore.
This time I am alone.
Maybe that's why my anguish goes unknown,
Why I suffered fever for a whole month?

He busies himself collecting the medicine
and doctors, yet all I wanted was the trust
to immune my heart and wounded soul.
The same applies to your situation,whole.

He still perceives you bliss, a tiny toddler,
Unaware of the growth with burden of fear.

PSYCHOLOGIST

When one door closes shut,
another beckons, revealing a new rut.
I am not getting a way out,
but that doesn't mean no one can.

I look for a person
who comprehends the pain.
I know the pain
yet lack mere experience.

But I need the one
who can help with the curative touch.
A well-versed mind,
capable of liberating you as such.

We are visiting the specialist,
a psychologist, with so much of my hopes.
It is no less than light
after dwelling in the darkest dome.

I place my trust in you,
as you yearn to leave this robe.
She instills belief,
you can shine after any door.

With hopes, I see the fear in you.
I see you crying, sharing from the crude.
You empathize with the pain of all,
from heinous assault to the crimes on call.

# The Sinking Hulk

You are afraid of manhood,
but baby, you should know
That can't be your route.
It is hard to see you this low.

This fear has made
the space in your core.
I wish it could go fade,
I wish I could do a little more.

Things haven't changed all yet,
but it's a hope… that we get.

# The Sinking Hulk

We go out for walks,
and feel the warmth of wet grass.
Sometimes for ice creams,
other times for a long talk.

Sharing the secrets of friends,
gossiping about some stupid trends,
emotions shared, lifting burdens down,
listening to tales we never thought to crown.

Every day with a hope
we went out with a skipping rope
we play, we laugh,
sometimes we cry yet enjoy our time.

We are no more just siblings
but the friends we were looking out for.
We hear, we suggest,
and we look at each other's side.

I no longer feel hopeless,
I see the dawn and then rays of light.
I look back and analyze
you never bore a responsibility I realize.

As you grow responsible and wise,
more senses to control, to analyze.
I ponder what charge to give you,
not so tiny, make you feel bad…

not so huge that burdens your head.
I'm afraid if you falter,
you'll be pushed to even darker.
I'm scared you'll be beyond my reach.

I offer you a piece of my heart,
the things I love the most.
They may get ruined, I'll manage.
*Narayana,* just make him grow.

Trust my belief. I yearn for your growth;
I'm glad you handle it and earn self-hope.

Di
Got it.
Bhai, u ok?
U ate?
My pulses were normal today
4 more days... Then we'll be together
Will uh cook Maggie for me?
Hm..
Good night bro ...
Good morning bhai..
Hope u r doing well.
Talked to psychologist?
Bro, why didn't u take therapy today?
No
I'm ok
Pick up my call.
Message

A month has passed,
I see you growing
but a moment comes,
a challenging split we face.

I test positive for COVID’s hold
relieved you all are safe, truth to be told.
I have to live away for days fourteen,
yet unsure if you’ll do self-care?

On calls and messages
I make sure you are motivated.
I hope for your wellness,
praying you don't succumb to carelessness.

It's a relief that you were healing,
and I hope it continues appealing.
All day in my room,
I think about if you are in the gloom.

On the phone, you sound fine.
When asked, you claim a good mood's line.
You say you study well,
and listen to everything *Mumma* tells.

But I doubt when
you stop attending video calls
and your reply shortens,
minimal at best, 'Hmm'.

## The Sinking Hulk

Those last five days
are like living in hell.
I keep waiting for this to end,
to see if you have the same strength.

I lay down in the dark,
feeling the era from the past.
Our stories might not be the same
but the similarity is in the pain.

Stay assured, you've someone to behold
but for how long, till the fate's told?

When I reach to you
and look at your smile.
To a moron,
it was no less than an extra life.

A long time after
we meet and get to sit together.
I was missing this so much,
but you are adrift in your own world.

I try to communicate,
but you have closed all gates.
I ask you directly,
but silence remains.

You spend all your time alone,
like a locked room in a home.
I am knocking it from out
no response, on calling for you so loud.

I question myself,
searching for the flaws,
'Do I need to restart
from that raw?'

I look around, finding no way.
It is like all the journeys we had,
has lost its aim.
My hope starts to fade.

# The Sinking Hulk

You have blocked all the holes,
leaving me far at poles.
I want to give up this time,
thinking let you handle your life.

My tears flow like endless rains
crying over your pain.
No matter how much I understand,
I guess pain can never be shared.

Feeling helpless, my hands tied.
Was I wrong to call it 'Our Fight'?

# The Sinking Hulk

A long time it takes,
but the clouds have dispersed.
The sky is clear, loam is wet,
the serene breeze whispers in my ear.

I remember all the words,
got up to leave you alone.
You hold my finger,
insisting for a little long.

I take my seat on damped soil,
'You know you are best,'
You say and smile.
Uncertain of how to respond, so keep quiet.

'When I was a child,
I don't remember much
yet I know you did so much for me.
*Mumma* says the first chapati you made,
was for me.'

I laugh, 'What else could I have done?
*Mumma* was sick, Dad was out,
back then we didn't have a maid,
so I stepped up for our aid.'

'Yeah, she told me I asked elders first
but all made excuses for being busy,
then you got up and made dough,
standing on a drum, for me.'

'Yeah, I was so short.
I guess I was just ten or eleven,
whatever thanks, you made me learn.'
'But you got that burn.'

You gaze at me with tearful eyes.
'You've always put effort, end up in pain,
Sorry, I just want to end this chain.
You are the best, no need to claim.'

'Sister, you are kind, deserving of ease,
No matter who it is, even your brother.'

# The Sinking Hulk

'Your heart is no harder than wax
but from your perspective it's just a burn.
You gave me love that is deep and true,
A love that encompasses the world too.'

'Why do you look so amazed?
It is not complicated.
You see the burns upon my skin,
but fails to perceive the love beneath.'

'Whenever my any effort
makes you smile,
It raised the confidence
and showed up in my shine.'

I have more to explain,
'Plus, do you remember,
What kind of food I gave you that day?'
You look around and move neck in NO.

'It was dreadful,
chapati had holes,
vegetable was in a lot of salt.'
You find it relatable with the present skills.

'Yet you ate like two or one
and said the food was *yumm*.
You praised it before our parents
and called me best sister from then.'

You put your head on my lap,
'You are my best sister
but I can trust your chapati with holes.
Years have gone, still, you cook horrible.'

We laugh, reminiscing
the days of childhood's bliss.
Your eyes still make me special.
It fills me with hope anew.

'You asked me to cook for you then,
but why can't you trust this grown-up
and share what's in your head?'

# The Sinking Hulk

'You know all that I think, but why me?
I am feeling that I hurt you.
I feel like I've raised your burden.
I should've dealt with it on my own.'

I want you to know I'm here,
but my presence never made any glare.
You get up and walk home.
I stay seated there till Father comes.

We greet and talk about the day,
'Father, why do we try to handle
everything when we know our strength?'
He smiled, 'Are you asking for brother?'

I don't say a word,
'He is finding his identity,
seeking for his place
among peers and within his own affinity.'

I keep listening to the wise,
'He is seeking a chance to prove himself,
and maybe the pandemic has put a limit.
He's filling his heart in different ways.'

'But there will come a time,
when you can't control.
Is it something like,
one is testing the self-role?'

'I can see him filling this way,
but I know the human range.
He'll be fine. Moreover, he is my son.'
He asks me not to worry and walks away.

All this leads me to one thing
so true, so valid
He is filling himself with some certain.
What if he crosses the mind range?

Something should be done to create a tear.
If he starts self-harm, it raised my fear.

# The Sinking Hulk

Flowing with time,
solitude has become prime.
Your ears seem used to my words,
like no need to take them or to hear.

I express love to make myself clear,
I scold at you till my throat is sore.
I hold your hand but you yank,
I am so worried about this flank.

I called your counselor,
but she is sick.
I tried everything but seems, no way out,
feeling so stuck in mid.

'What are you thinking?
Why are you confused?
You should be motivated
yet you are getting rude.'

You yell at me,
and this time, you hurt.
You are a person who knows care and love,
I really want you to clear this dirt.

The pain in you has tasted the rage.
I can see you filled up to the brim.
Please, Baby! Come out of this cage
and understand my concern.

## The Sinking Hulk

The more I try, the more you yell.
You don't listen to what I want to tell.
Each pore of my body is crying,
the fire in you is trapping me in hell.

I curse life and hate myself,
for being futile, this much useless.
I've tried all my ways with full strength,
seems nothing left for you on my shelf.

I thought I will hold you all my life.
Now I feel so small, so little,
maybe craving to behold this time.

# The Sinking Hulk

A long night after,
our father came to us.
He sits beside you,
resting his arm upon your shoulder.

He asks why you have grown colder,
with reassurance, he claims his watchful eye.
You are just listening to him staying quiet,
but I wish you could respond more buoyant.

## The Sinking Hulk

He keeps saying looking at your face,
desiring some semblance of a breakthrough.
I can feel him, seeing you rude these days,
I've felt belittled many times the same way.

You play with a crystal hulk, lost in thought
Passing, from hand to hand, feeling fraught.
He asks, 'Son, what is troubling you so?'
'There is nothing. I'm tired of this all.'

His patience should not be tested.
He snatches green crystal from your hand
and break it into two pieces,
taking out its wooden stand.

He walks out of our room.
I follow him, after telling you what to do.
You walk fast to catch him soon
and apologize with lowered eyes.

# The Sinking Hulk

You lie again, 'Dad I'm fine'
but the man has faith in his eyes.
'Son, the wrinkles I got aren't due to stress,
So don't try to be so hard,
as if you can suppress.'

He sees the toy pieces carefully,
and hold your hand tight,
Take you in his bathroom.
I follow you both, praying for the right.

I am scared of how you will take this,
but deep down, I know my father is wise.

# The Sinking Hulk

He drops the Hulk
in a tub filled with water.
The water spills with loud voice.
I want to react but choose to be quiet.

He asks you to tell him what has happened.
You look at him to know what's the matter.
He insists you, ‘explain with voice.’
You come up with, 'my hulk is in water.'

He then drops the wooden piece.
It makes noise but does not much spill.
He looks at you and asks you to describe.
You lean against the wall,
'Dad now the wood is on water.'

He came out and sat on the chair.
You look at him, waiting for words to clear.
I take out the immersed pair.
feeling confident I've understood it so fair.

He looks at me and smiles,
and gestures to sit near.
I rest on the corner of the bed
while you pick and analyze the broken toy.

'Child!' he addresses me with love,
'What happens when crystal goes in water?'
'Dad, it made the more water out,
with so much noise.'

Now he moves to you to hear your words,
You now see, there could be
a lot more than just a broken toy.
You look at him and sit in his front.

'I didn't think that way,
but yes! sister is right.
Why are we discussing it this way?
It's still so morning.' I see you smile bright.

Long time after, I see you both laughing.
looking at each other,
            adoring being wise and one so naive.

# The Sinking Hulk

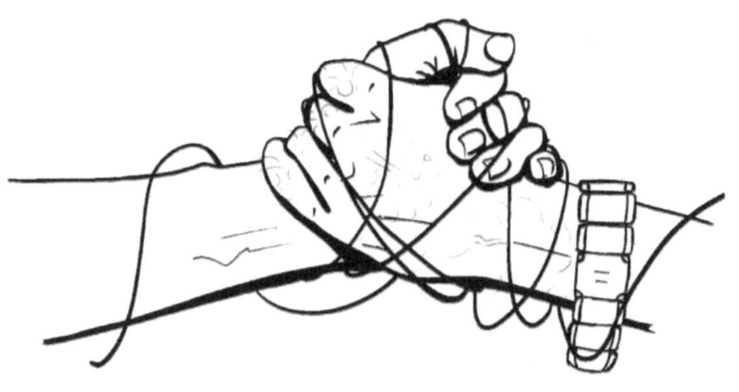

‘Son, if I'm not mistaken,
*Huluk* is the one in that movie we saw.'
Dad again mispronounces, teasing you in jest
knowing that it brings forth a playful jest.

'Dad it's Hulk, not *Huluk*.
Yes, he is in the movie *Avenger*.'
You seem annoyed
but you know he does it for fun.

'Kid, no matter how strong he may be,
the crystal sank when immersed
but the wood floats
which counted to have no role.'

I'm amazed by the depth of his words
and listen intently to everything he says.
His words are true,
I'm trying to see his motive through.

You stay silent,
looking into his eyes.
I'm happy that you have learned
to adore the wisdom of the wise.

He looks at me and keeps saying,
'No matter how strong you are,
you need a base to rest and stay calm.
Crystal sinks so needs a wooden stand.'

'Son, you can't handle everything,
you'll sink on keep filling yourself this way,
surely now you know what I mean,
you need a family to hold you. Mean it.'

I grin to know how easy it was,
with wisdom in the way he shared
A message of love and family values,
A message that you are his son.

You look calm and happy, to know
the man you trust is there to behold.

# The Sinking Hulk

On that dusky evening,
I lie down on the grass green.
I am relieved to know
that I'm not alone.

The same moment you arrive
you greet and set aside.
'Thanks for being my wooden stand,'
you say with your eyes on the sky.

Though I never expected that,
stay silent to know you more.
'Sister, I read your words.
You had a moment where you sank.'

You keep saying while my tears rolled.
'I couldn't know how to handle this threat
and unintentionally I hurt you, I mistreat.
There is no difference... I am a man.'

You lowered your eyes
but can't meet mine.
'Baby, yes! you are a man,
You can't help it.'

My words may have hurt you,
but I can't resist telling the truth.
'The man, who has some values,
the one who has the guts to apologize.'

I hold your face with both my hands,
looking eyes, I make my stand.
'You have a heart that only a man can hold,
those were demons I was scared of.

Though I'm strong now, I've healed my side
I don't want you to be a man to shield me
but my boy, be a person who can see a soul,
who can be a strong wall to every wrong.'

'You can't hurt anyone even in your dream.
You've to nourish yourself with self-belief.'

# The Sinking Hulk

'You are sensitive. You are kind.
Please love your heart and trust your mind.
You can't survive if you don't adore self,
I don't want you to be a machine.'

I mean every word I say.
I feel the warm soul behind the flesh.
You can live without the tears.
You can win every pain with your grace.

'How can you smile
with so much pain inside?'
'I don't have any hidden pain,
I left that all so far, so behind.'

'I was young, I wobbled many times.
Yet I just keep believing in myself.
Same way, I managed to handle my cries.
I don't blame anyone, it is just self-pride.'

I can see the same pride for me
in your eyes and smile.
This is what I've earned
after years of hard work and self-trust.

'Sister, you held the same trust in me.
I don't know how long it will take.
Please stay with me, I want to make it.
I'm into the water, looking for self-trust.

Be my wooden stand
until I reach the land.'
I see the seeds of confidence
sowing in the sod of self-love.

I see the little boy
growing to become a whole world.
I am sure it won't fade away.
This time your soul is leading the way.

I rest my head on your shoulder.
Dad, I took care of the baby with my best,
I hope you don't regret.

# The Sinking Hulk

## Dear Teenager,

How easy it was when you were a kid. You didn't have any anxieties, worries, obligations, peer pressure, or pimples, of course. All you had to do was eat, sleep, weep, and poop. Everything was extremely simple.

Right?

Truth be told, NO.

You were safe in your mother's womb. You grew up hoping to experience this world.

When you came out, the first and the worst you had to do was to inhale. Can you picture yourself in your mother's womb not needing to breathe or eat but suddenly having to fight for life?

The very first second after birth you had to struggle for a breath. You were crying when the air first entered your nostrils and traveled through all of your untouched veins to reach your lungs. However, you could do that because you were brave.

You did it.

You learned to cry. You learned to feed yourself.

You held your *Mumma's* finger and raised yourself to your feet.

You did it.

Same thing now,

If you want to achieve your goal, you need to start working. It is impossible to sit and wish for something to happen.

You must get up and move forward at your own pace. You have to face all the difficulties for sure. You cannot blame all the time for everything you didn't work for.

You are unique. Since your approaches are distinctive, it stands to reason that your challenges and strategies for solving them would be as well. You are the answer to every problem you see.

I know, sometimes you feel like... you are alone, and your family and friends don't understand you. So why can't you accompany yourself rather than become sidetracked?

Why can't you instruct yourself and lead yourself in the right direction to achieve the goal?

Hiding yourself, isolating yourself, or giving up can never be an answer to any of your problems.

What gave you the impression that if you close your eyes, the issues will resolve themselves? That will remain there staring at you and your weaknesses unless you confront it.

A teenager once asked me, 'What if I don't have any goal? I don't know what I should do. Even though I am unsure about my abilities, what can I do?'

Whenever you question yourself, ask yourself what you can't do.

See what challenges are waiting for you.

Welcome every challenge and jump out of your comfort zone. Experiment with new things.

Just make sure you are not hurting humanity and to avoid that, you need to be your own behold.

In a world, full of opportunities, the challenge you found is exactly what you were looking for.

# The Sinking Hulk

Only a dancer experiences trouble with a specific dance or move. The efforts to cross the finish line within a set amount of time are only experienced by swimmers.

Speaking for myself, I find the editing process to be lazy. Only writers are aware of the difficulties involved in book authoring.

Pal, life has never been easy and it never will be. It is just the beginning.

If you wobble at this point only, how will you continue this journey?

How will you succeed in the future?

More the difficulty you face, the more pleasurous the results will be.

So... stay positive, stay self-motivated, stay calm, and face everything that you thought you can't, and this time with grace.

Don't trust me or anyone else.

Trust yourself.

YOU CAN AND YOU WILL.

## Dear Parents,

When you held your child for the first time, you were happy and nervous but you were also determined that no matter what happens, you will take care of your child and give them the best life possible. Starting that day, you keep running, you keep earning to give your child the kind of upbringing you had always envisioned. You work hard to provide everything for your child to make both the present and the future easy and comfortable, from the best food to the best clothing, from the best school to the greatest sports. You give up all of your dreams to give your child the ability to glimpse the fantasy world. To encourage your child to pursue all of their interests, you gave up all of your passions. To be honest, having parents around itself is a blessing of Lord Narayana for a child.

But why?

Have you ever questioned yourself why you are doing this for your child?

Some will say, “It’s my child.”

Some will say, “My child will be the stick of my old age.

Some will say, “It is our culture.”

And some will say, “My child, will live the life of dreams that I couldn't.”

Don't you think, in the race for earnings and giving them what you desire, you are ignoring their needs and desire?

You are placing a heavy burden on your child’s shoulders by telling him or her to find love in worldly possessions.

You are busy earning while your child is yearning for love and affection. You keep working hard while your child learns to disrespect what you earn. You keep struggling while your child cries alone in the dark.

I'm not here to question or criticize your parenting, but as a child, I am aware of the challenges young one encounters in the outside world. Every time they notice that you are not there for them at that point, the distance you established grows.

You always expect that your child can't do any wrong. You raised them in order to provide for them, but you never had a time when the child wanted to be with you. You were busy when he or she needed your attention. You imposed what you wanted. You expect them to do as you wish, because you gave birth to them, are raising them, or are meeting all of their needs.

A kid in conversation once said, 'I am nothing more than a tool for my parents to use for their future.'

This phrase made me incredibly sad but also explains the gap between the child and his parents. It is not a single child's narrative. These days, so many kids share that sentiment.

So, it is a request that you give your child the time that is required. Play with them, read with them, assist them with their homework, explore new dimensions with them, and discover new things to open their doors of learning and generate positivity around your child.

And watch out that you don't forget about yourself. Since every child's home serves as their first classroom, children learn from their parents. If you give up on your dreams, the youngsters will quickly absorb this lesson and learn to give up easily.

A child is a blessing, not a hindrance.

A child is precious, not an investment for the future.

# The Sinking Hulk

## *From the pen of an expert*

*People around the world are depressed, anxious, and stressed some more than others. With the COVID-19 pandemic spreading across the globe, health organizations are calling on individuals to maintain good hygiene, practice social distancing and stay at home. While protecting physical health may be a top priority, attention should be given to the mental health outgrowth of the current situation. A major component weighing on their well-being is the isolation they are experiencing as they remain alone with their thoughts.*

*What is it about the isolation that makes us so anxious? The answer is multilayered, touching, among other things on distressing thoughts and beliefs emotional regulation, and the social roles we identify.*

*The greatest impacts felt by adolescents stem from school closures, and being in the house with family and peers. Teenagers are at a stage in life when they are very invested in separating from their parents. So, pandemic social distancing requirements have a different emotional impact on them. Parents can reassure them that it is not likely to make them seriously sick if they do not have underlying conditions that put them at risk. At the same time communicate the importance of them playing their part in keeping other people safe.*

*Family plays a critical role in helping teenagers to cope with the stress of the pandemic. There are strategies parents can engage to help, whether or not their teen is showing signs of problems.*

*One of the most important things for parents to do is keep lines of communication open; ask their teens how they are doing and create the space for them to speak honestly so they can provide help when needed. Teenagers are suffering from anxiety issues, thinking, etc.*

*There are several different types of anxiety problems as disorders:*

*a) Social phobia, social anxiety disorder, or the fear of social situations or of being judged or embarrassed in public.*

*b) Generalized anxiety disorder.*

*c) Specific phobias or intense fears of dogs or heights.*

*d) Panic disorder: Panic disorder is repeated, unexpected panic attacks. A panic attack is an overwhelming feeling of fear or panic in a situation where most people wouldn't be afraid.*

*e) Agoraphobia refers to situations where it might be hard to escape or get help if things go wrong.*

*f) Separation anxiety disorder or SAD is an excessive fear of being separated from home or a loved one.*

*Your child might not want to talk with you about how they're feeling. Your child might even say there's nothing wrong. Your child might not want to talk with you about how they're feeling. Your child might even say there's nothing wrong. You play an important role in helping your child to develop confidence in their ability to overcome anxieties.*

*There are many ways you can support your child with an anxiety disorder and look after your child's mental health at home.*

*a) Acknowledge your child's fear – don't dismiss or ignore it. Let your child know you're there to support and care for them.*

*b) Gently encourage your child to do the things that they're anxious about. But don't force them.*

*c) Praise your child for doing something they feel anxious about.*

*d) Avoid labeling your child as 'shy' or 'anxious'. Try to refer to your child as 'brave' or another positive term. Your child is trying to overcome their difficulties.*

*Overthinking involves focusing on the negative rehashing the past, dwelling on bad experiences, or worrying about the future. Overthinking becomes a problem when it starts to affect everyday life. Some of my patients who deal with negative thoughts and anxiety have also experienced headaches, body aches, and stomach problems. Overthinking is also often associated with mental health issues like depression, anxiety, post-traumatic stress, and borderline personality disorder.*

*To break the habit, a good first step is to take note of what triggers your overthinking. It might stem from a past trauma or something in your life that's currently a source of stress.*

*Once you identify those triggers. You can start finding ways to overcome them.*

*Some Tips To Stop Overthinking:-*

*a) Notice when you are thinking too much.*

*b) Challenge negative thoughts. Acknowledge that they may be exaggerated.*

*c) Focus on problem-solving. Dwelling on problems is not helpful, seeking a solution is.*
*d) Schedule time for reflection. If you start overthinking outside that time, tell yourself you will save it for later.*
*e) Practice mindfulness.*
*Always remember, only a positive mind can give you a positive life.*

*Ms. Kamakshi*
*(Counseling Psychologist)*
*(Founder of Enchanted Self)*

Hope this read will strengthen the bond, you care for.

Take a few minutes for a book review as well.

It helps our growth.

Your Rating: ☆☆☆☆☆

Your favorite lines:

Your Thoughts:

Use #thesinkinghulk

www.ingramcontent.com/pod-product-compliance
Lightning Source LLC
La Vergne TN
LVHW091208150826
845672LV00005B/1282

* 9 7 8 9 3 5 9 8 0 1 8 8 9 *